MIGHTY MACHINES
IN ACTION

Trains

by Chris Bowman

BELLWETHER MEDIA · MINNEAPOLIS, MN

Note to Librarians, Teachers, and Parents:

Blastoff! Readers are carefully developed by literacy experts and combine standards-based content with developmentally appropriate text.

Level 1 provides the most support through repetition of high-frequency words, light text, predictable sentence patterns, and strong visual support.

Level 2 offers early readers a bit more challenge through varied simple sentences, increased text load, and less repetition of high-frequency words.

Level 3 advances early-fluent readers toward fluency through increased text and concept load, less reliance on visuals, longer sentences, and more literary language.

Level 4 builds reading stamina by providing more text per page, increased use of punctuation, greater variation in sentence patterns, and increasingly challenging vocabulary.

Level 5 encourages children to move from "learning to read" to "reading to learn" by providing even more text, varied writing styles, and less familiar topics.

Whichever book is right for your reader, Blastoff! Readers are the perfect books to build confidence and encourage a love of reading that will last a lifetime!

This edition first published in 2017 by Bellwether Media, Inc.

No part of this publication may be reproduced in whole or in part without written permission of the publisher. For information regarding permission, write to Bellwether Media, Inc., Attention: Permissions Department, 5357 Penn Avenue South, Minneapolis, MN 55419.

Library of Congress Cataloging-in-Publication Data

Names: Bowman, Chris, 1990- author.
Title: Trains / by Chris Bowman.
Description: Minneapolis, MN : Bellwether Media, Inc., 2017. | Series:
   Blastoff! Readers. Mighty Machines in Action | Audience: Ages 5-8. |
   Audience: K to grade 3. | Includes bibliographical references and index.
Identifiers: LCCN 2016033336 (print) | LCCN 2016046863 (ebook) | ISBN
   9781626176102 (hardcover : alk. paper) | ISBN 9781681033402 (ebook)
Subjects: LCSH: Railroad trains–Juvenile literature.
Classification: LCC TF148 .B692 2017 (print) | LCC TF148 (ebook) | DDC
   625.1–dc23
LC record available at https://lccn.loc.gov/2016033336

Editor: Christina Leighton   Designer: Jon Eppard

Printed in the United States of America, North Mankato, MN.

Table of Contents

People gather at the station.
They are ready to ride a
high-speed train.

They board and find a seat. Then the train is ready to go.

The train gathers speed. Soon,
it is going nearly 100 miles
(161 kilometers) per hour!

It zooms past many places. Then the train slows. It has arrived!

cargo

Trains are found in cities and the countryside. Some carry **cargo** long distances.

Other trains bring people from one place to another.

THE WORLD'S FASTEST TRAIN
Shanghai Maglev

Top Speed: 267 miles (430 kilometers) per hour
Trip Time: about 8 minutes
Trip Distance: 19 miles (30 kilometers)
Location: China

Some trains work below ground. Subways carry people around cities.

Others work on mountains.
They bring people up and
down steep slopes.

LOCOMOTIVES, CARS, AND TRACKS

Locomotives power many trains. They often have **diesel engines**.

locomotive

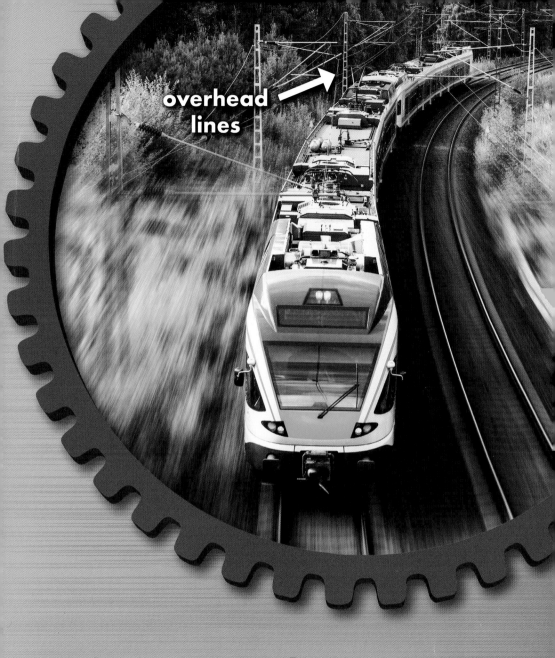

overhead
lines

Other trains use **electricity**.
Power comes from overhead
lines or a third rail.

Trains are made up of cars that are **coupled** together.

THE LONGEST
PASSENGER TRAIN
The Ghan

length: 3,596 feet (1,096 meters)

The Ghan

football field

Cars: 44

Locomotives: 2

Location: Australia

caboose

Many trains used to have a **caboose**. Now, a red light usually marks the end.

Trains follow tracks
with one or more rails.

rails

railroad ties

Some trains roll over **railroad ties**. Others speed above **magnets**.

Train drivers sit in a **cab**. They control the speed and watch out for other trains.

IDENTIFY A TRAIN

cars

cab

7450 7450

7450

BNSF

7444 BNSF

locomotive

tracks

cab

switch

Switches allow trains to pass one another.

Trains have been used for more than 200 years.

Whether they carry people or cargo, trains are still an important way to travel!

Glossary

cab—the part of the train where the driver sits

caboose—the railroad car at the back of the train

cargo—something that is carried by a train

coupled—connected together

diesel engines—loud engines that burn diesel fuel and are often used in big machines

electricity—energy carried through wires

locomotives—vehicles with engines that pull railroad cars

magnets—pieces of metal that attract other pieces of metal; magnets are sometimes used to move trains.

railroad ties—beams that are underneath the rails to support them

switches—places where trains can move from one track to another

To Learn More

AT THE LIBRARY
Carr, Aaron. *Trains.* New York, N.Y.: AV2 by Weigl, 2016.

Silverman, Buffy. *How Do Trains Work?* Minneapolis, Minn.: Lerner Publications, 2016.

Spaight, Anne J. *Trains on the Go.* Minneapolis, Minn.: Lerner Publications, 2017.

ON THE WEB
Learning more about trains
is as easy as 1, 2, 3.

1. Go to www.factsurfer.com.

2. Enter "trains" into the search box.

3. Click the "Surf" button and you will see a
   list of related web sites.

With factsurfer.com, finding more
information is just a click away.

Index